Oseola McCarty

Oseola McCarty's

Simple Wisdom
for Rich Living

OSEOLA MCCARTY'S

Simple Wisdom for Rich Living

LONGSTREET PRESS
Atlanta, Georgia

Published by
LONGSTREET PRESS, INC.
A subsidiary of Cox Newspapers,
A subsidiary of Cox Enterprises, Inc.
2140 Newmarket Parkway
Suite 118
Marietta, GA 30067

2nd printing 1996

Printed in the United States of America

Library of Congress Card Catalog Number: 96-76509

ISBN: 1-56352-341-8

Jacket and book design by Jill Dible
Jacket photo by Steve Coleman

In memory of my grandmother, Julia Smith McCarty,
my mother, Lucy McCarty Zinerman,
and my aunt, Evelyn McCarty

Contents

Acknowledgments

African American Student Organization
Berthe Amoss
Woodrow Armstrong
Virginia Borghese
Cynthia Eiland
The University of Southern Mississippi Foundation —
Board of Directors
Phil Hearn
Lewis Katz
William E. "Bud" Kirkpatrick
Lower Adirondack Arts Council
Paul Laughlin
Aubrey K. Lucas
Mary McCarty
J. F. McKenzie

Nancy Odom
Bill Pace
Jeannine Porter
Gayle Rose
Eric Suben
J. T. Tisdale
Jewel Tucker
Ellen Vinzant
The Women's Foundation of Greater Memphis —
Virginia Dunaway, Executive Director

Special thanks to editor Shannon Maggio who knows all
the right words . . . and how to cook vegetables, too.

Introduction

Sitting on the front porch eating vanilla ice cream, we talk when the traffic is not roaring by. Traffic is the only noise on this quiet porch and quiet day, in a life that is no longer quiet.

Oseola McCarty's life is filled with the sounds of applause and proclamations of praise. (Her crystal awards clink together on her dining room table if you walk too heavily across the floor.) She has grown accustomed to the roar of jet engines, the hum of tape recorders, and the lights of television cameras.

But two years ago Oseola McCarty says she "was just a little old colored woman who walked everywhere." Nobody paid any attention to her. Nobody smiled at her. It was a life of routine and simple duty, of faith and faithfulness, of aloneness and obscurity. It had never been any different.

Oseola McCarty started working and saving at a very young age. Beginning when she was eight, she spent her after-school hours washing and ironing beside her mother, grandmother, and aunt to help make ends meet. Later, when illness limited her aunt's ability to work, Oseola had to fill an earnings gap for the household. She quit school in the sixth grade and went to work full time. She never made it back to the classroom.

In the place of education, work became the great good of her life. She found beauty in its movement and pride in its provisions. She was happy to have it and gave herself over to it with abandon — sometimes staying up until two or three in the morning to finish her ironing. There was little else that captivated her. She did not desire possessions or travel. She wanted only her God, her work, and her family. Fortunately, she had all three in abundance.

Oseola was baptized when she was thirteen. She remembers the event in vivid detail — dressing all in white, walking down to the pond, and being dunked under the water. Her faith in the God she chose that day has never wavered. She believes in His supreme goodness and beneficence toward humanity and receives His particular love for her with joy. She looks to Jesus as an example for behavior and trusts that because she does, she will be blessed. Her faith is as simple as the Sermon on the Mount and as difficult to practice.

In her adult years, it was faith that sustained Oseola through the greatest trials of her life: the loss of her grandmother in 1944, her mother in 1964, and her aunt in 1967. Those three women had been her nuturers, housemates, coworkers, and confidantes since her birth. Their absence left her alone in the world.

But the work went on until 1994, when arthritis forced Miss McCarty to retire at age 86. Friends at Trustmark Bank, where she had deposited her monthly savings her entire working life, encouraged her to begin planning for care, should she need it, and for the management of her property after death. During those planning sessions, Oseola revealed the wild idea that had been burgeoning in her soul for many years — giving some of the money she had quietly and slowly accumulated to her church and family but most of it to the local college, the University of Southern Mississippi.

After bank officers had consulted with Miss McCarty's

attorney and she had signed an irrevocable trust agreement, her gift to the school was announced in July 1995. The news shocked school officials and later the world. Oseola McCarty, washerwoman, had saved $280,000 over the course of her lifetime and had given $150,000 to a school she had never even visited. In August, Stephanie Bullock, an 18-year-old African-American Hattiesburg High School honor graduate, became the first Oseola McCarty Scholarship recipient. Miss McCarty had made sure that others would have the education she was denied.

Since the announcement, Oseola McCarty has had a new kind of work to do. She spends much of her time giving interviews or traveling to receive awards. She has appeared on ABC, CNN, NBC, BET, and MTV, and she has been featured in *Newsweek*, the *New York Times*, *People*, *Life*, *Ebony*, *Essence*, and *Jet*. Her numerous national and international awards include the Presidential Citizens Medal, the Wallenberg Humanitarian Award, and the Avicenna Medal from UNESCO.

The sudden fame has not changed Miss McCarty. She remains unaffected and gentle, and she speaks only what she knows, an understanding gained through a simple, work-filled life. It might be difficult to imagine that Miss McCarty has a type of wisdom relevant to the '90s, until one considers what life is really all about. She has lived life on its essential levels and lived it well. She has grown up, gone to work, taken care of family, paid her bills, worshipped her God, and grown older. Few people ever get beyond making it, but she has made it better — for Stephanie Bullock and untold numbers in the future.

The strength to accept life as it comes and the vision to make it more than what it seems must come from somewhere. In the case of Oseola McCarty, it came from within. *Simple Wisdom for Rich Living* reveals the principles that shaped her exemplary life and character. Like faith, they are very simple to comprehend, but incredibly hard to practice. That is no surprise. Saints and heroes earn their status by doing what the rest of us won't, one lifetime at a time.

— Shannon Maggio

Oseola McCarty's

Simple Wisdom for Rich Living

Oseola McCarty as a young woman.

On
Work

*T*hrough unfortunate circumstances, (at least unfortunate by most of people's standards) Oseola McCarty became involved in the family laundry business at age eight. Although that involvement cost Miss McCarty a formal education, it instilled in her a work ethic that she never abandoned. For almost eighty years, she actually took pride in doing laundry.

I have heard her describe in almost poetic terms the laundry process of her daily routine.

When I was working, I would wake up at seven. I would go outside and start building a fire under my wash pot. Then I would soak, wash, and boil a bundle of clothes. Then I would rub them, wrench them, rub them again, starch 'em, and hang 'em on the line. After I had all of the clean clothes on the line, I would start on the next batch. By the time they were finished washing, the clothes on the line would be dry. I'd take them down and pile them up in the house, on the beds, or wherever there was an open spot. Well, I would wash all day, and in the evenings I would iron until eleven o'clock.

I loved the work. The bright fire. Wrenching the wet, clean cloth. White shirts shining on the line.

Apparently, some of her customers hold her work in similar esteem. I know one person who still has several shirts that were last cleaned almost two years ago by Miss McCarty. He says that he does not intend to wear them; he just takes them out periodically to look at them and to enjoy the crisp fabric and its scent.

— Paul Laughlin

Paul Laughlin is Vice President and Trust Officer at Trustmark Bank in Hattiesburg, Missisippi. He was the first person in whom McCarty confided her plans for establishing the scholarship. He continues to assist her with some of her financial decisions and much of her correspondence.

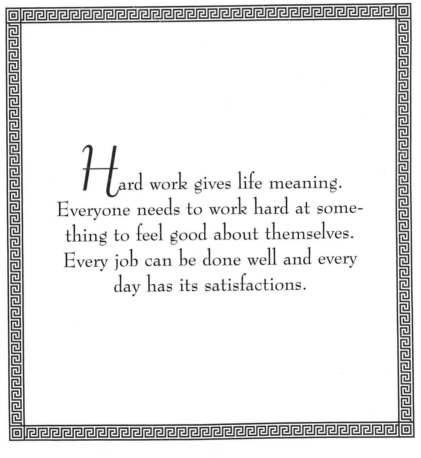

*H*ard work gives life meaning. Everyone needs to work hard at something to feel good about themselves. Every job can be done well and every day has its satisfactions.

I knew there were people who didn't have to work as hard as I did, but it didn't make me feel sad. I loved to work, and when you love to do anything, those things don't bother you. I just loved the work.

I was working to have my own things. Whatever it was. If it wasn't nothing but a piece of paper. That's just my makeup. I wanted something of my own. A sense of ownership was my satisfaction.

*P*eople complain all the time about how busy they are, but there is time enough for all the things that a person really wants to do. When I was working, I got only three or four hours of sleep each night. Sometimes I worked straight through for two or three days. I had goals I was working toward. That motivated me and I was able to push hard.

I don't believe in retirement. If I were able, I would still be working today. Work is a blessing. As long as I am living, I want to be working at something. Just because I am old doesn't mean I can't work.

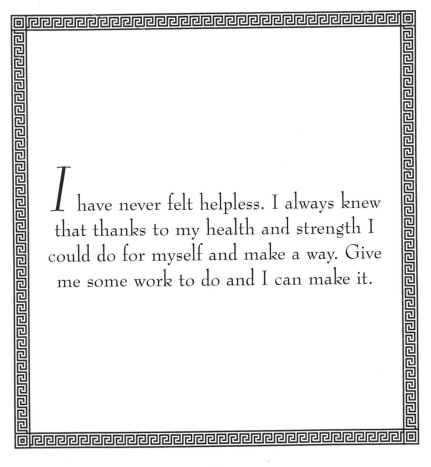

I have never felt helpless. I always knew that thanks to my health and strength I could do for myself and make a way. Give me some work to do and I can make it.

We are responsible for the way we use our time on this earth, so I try to be a good steward. I start each day on my knees, saying the Lord's Prayer. Then I get busy about my work. I get to cleaning or washing. I find that my life and my work are increasing all the time. I am blessed beyond what I hoped.

Every now and then, we would get tired of the routine of washing clothes, so we would sing or tell stories. Sometimes we went to the soda fountain or to a movie for entertainment. The change of pace always did me good.

A young Oseola McCarty (third from right) with family and friends in Hattiesburg, Mississippi, ca. 1922.

On
Saving
Money

Many people have wondered how Miss McCarty could have saved as much money as she did taking in laundry. There has been some speculation that she must have resorted to welfare or tax fraud. This unfortunate conclusion is a result of ignorance—ignorance about the time value of money and the character of Oseola McCarty.

Even as her banker, I did not understand the depth of Miss McCarty's conviction about saving until I escorted her to an out-of-town event. As we walked through the hotel lobby, she stopped dead in her tracks. When I asked her what was wrong, she pointed at a nearby fountain, the bottom of which was lined with coins. I explained that some people traditionally toss coins into fountains for good luck. She stood silent for a moment, wagging her head in utter disbelief. To Oseola McCarty there is no such thing as an insignificant amount of money.

Miss McCarty did not save a large amount over a short period of time; instead, she set aside a little bit, regularly, over a long period of time. She found ways to

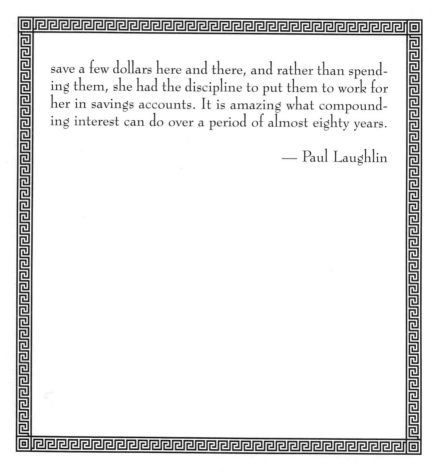

save a few dollars here and there, and rather than spending them, she had the discipline to put them to work for her in savings accounts. It is amazing what compounding interest can do over a period of almost eighty years.

— Paul Laughlin

I started saving when I was a little girl just to have candy money. When I got grown, I started saving for my future. I'd go to the bank once a month, hold out just enough to cover my expenses, and put the rest into my savings account. Every month I'd save the same and put it away. I was consistent.

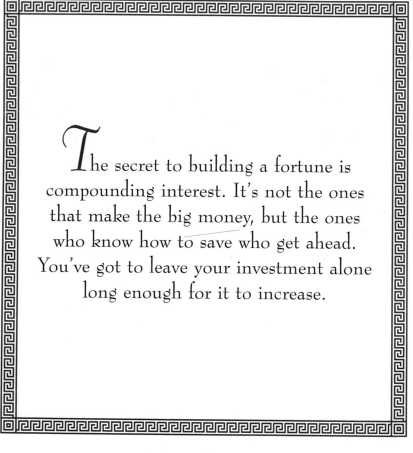

*T*he secret to building a fortune is compounding interest. It's not the ones that make the big money, but the ones who know how to save who get ahead. You've got to leave your investment alone long enough for it to increase.

I did have some advantages to saving money. My house was given to me by my uncle, and the people I worked for gave me clothes. I had to pay only for groceries and the other little things I needed. But I think my secret was contentment. I was happy with what I had.

I haven't always had enough money. There were times when we had to do without, but we never went hungry. The white people we worked for gave us left-over food. We would make a meal out of that meat and syrup and the vegetables we had put up. I learned that there is always a way to live.

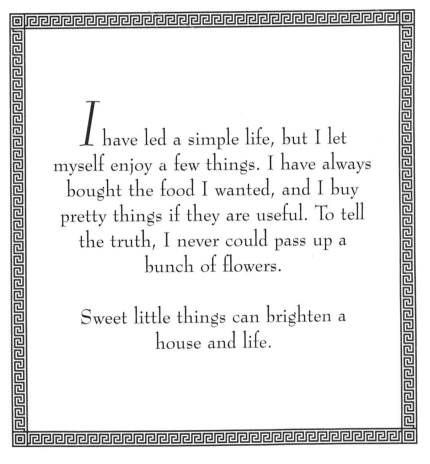

I have led a simple life, but I let myself enjoy a few things. I have always bought the food I wanted, and I buy pretty things if they are useful. To tell the truth, I never could pass up a bunch of flowers.

Sweet little things can brighten a house and life.

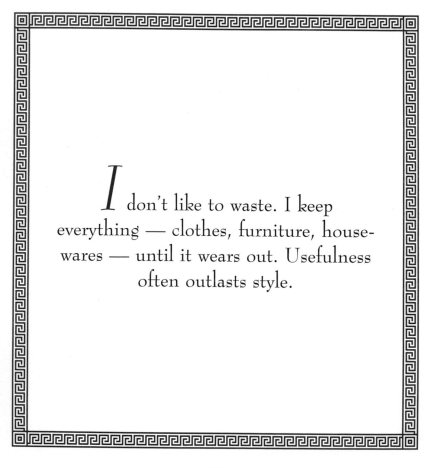

I don't like to waste. I keep everything — clothes, furniture, housewares — until it wears out. Usefulness often outlasts style.

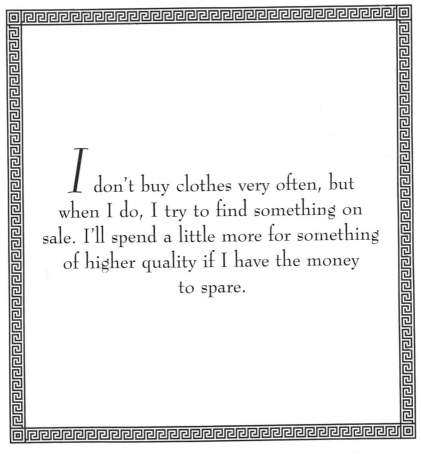

I don't buy clothes very often, but when I do, I try to find something on sale. I'll spend a little more for something of higher quality if I have the money to spare.

I don't spend a lot of money on electricity. I turn on the lights only when it's dark and I run the air conditioner only when it's really hot. Otherwise, I feel like I am throwing money out the window.

I do put some major purchases on credit. With my first payment, I cover half of the cost. But I pay out my bill by the end of the first month before they start charging interest. I save up my money until I can buy something outright.

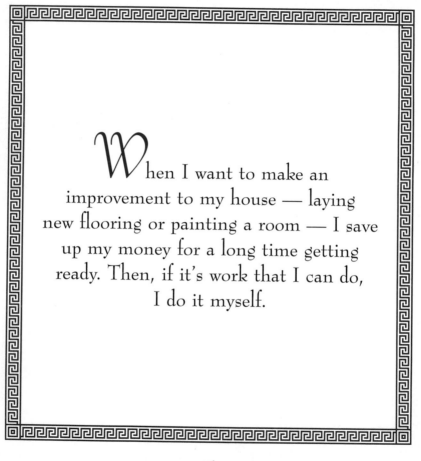

When I want to make an improvement to my house — laying new flooring or painting a room — I save up my money for a long time getting ready. Then, if it's work that I can do, I do it myself.

I visited a casino once and could not believe what I saw. People were lined up to put their change in those machines. I can tell you, gambling is like walking down to the river and throwing your money in the water. I don't want any part of that!

I think a Christmas savings account is a good idea. Every year I save and prepare to spend that money. It's crazy the way some people will get into debt at that time of year.

Credit cards are okay for some people, but I wouldn't go for one. I try not to spend money that I don't have buying what I can't afford.

$\mathcal{M}$y black and white television set gets only one channel. I don't care because I don't watch it often. I have never subscribed to a newspaper because it costs too much. There is a difference between needing and wanting. I don't need those things in my life. Other people may, but I don't.

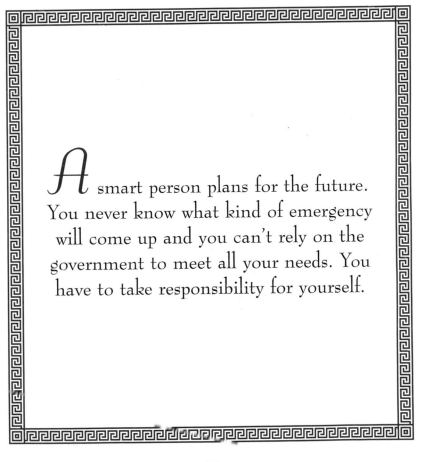

A smart person plans for the future. You never know what kind of emergency will come up and you can't rely on the government to meet all your needs. You have to take responsibility for yourself.

Oseola McCarty's mother, Lucy McCarty Zinerman, with her husband, Willy Zinerman, who died when Oseola was a young child, ca. 1926.

On
Faith

*I*n mid-June 1995, Bill Pace, the University of Southern Mississippi's director of development, stopped me in the hallway of the student union to tell me that a very elderly African-American woman in Hattiesburg had donated $150,000 of her life savings to the university. He made it clear that she was extremely shy and would probably not be open to much publicity. University president Dr. Aubrey K. Lucas hoped the school would get some good state press and maybe a story in the *Chronicle of Higher Education*.

Little did we know.

Overnight Miss McCarty became a media sensation. The quiet, private woman who had not had anyone to talk to for thirty years was suddenly making conversation with Barbara Walters and Bryant Gumbel and the President of the United States.

One year later, requests for interviews and announcements of awards in her honor are still arriving. She accepts every invitation she can, and on each occasion she proves to be a remarkable woman. She has handled the transition from obscurity to public life with disarming grace.

Several people have wondered aloud to me how she managed so well. Actually, the secret to her success is no secret at all. Miss McCarty has tackled the challenges of the interview in the same way she has taken on the rest of life. She is simply living out her faith in God. She is living out putting God first and trusting that all else will be added to her. She is living out her belief that for every step she takes, God will take two. As she says it, "I know He will. I know cause I have tried that, and it works."

— Bud Kirkpatrick

Bud Kirkpatrick has been Director of Public Relations at the Univesity of Southern Mississippi for thrity-eight years. Oseola McCarty's activities have been managed by his office for the past year.

I know people who don't know God just can't understand that He's real. Hearing the gospel means nothing to them because their ears aren't open. But the greatest lesson of faith I know is that you have to be willing to grow in grace. You have to be willing to start at the beginning and become like a child. You have to accept God the best way you know how and then He'll show Himself to you. And the more you serve Him, the more able you are to serve Him.

I think the way we live matters, not just for now but for always. There is an eternal side to everything you do. You can't lead just any kind of life and enter heaven. You have got to lead a clean life — take care of your responsibilities and be fair to people. I realize that some people have different beliefs, but I think you have got to have faith in Jesus and practice good works to get to heaven.

What I want people to know about Jesus is that there was nothing but love in Him. Even when they nailed His hands and feet, He was loving. It helps to think about that when going through hard times.

I have never been mad at or questioned God. He is above all our questions. People forget that. They forget that He is God and we are the work of His hands. He can do what He pleases.

$\mathcal{P}$eople are wrong to be tearing up the Bible. It means the same today that it meant yesterday. There's nothing new under the sun. Everything that is happening now was going on then. It can still tell us how we should live.

*McCarty's uncle, John McCarty, and her grandmother, Julia
Smith McCarty, ca. 1931.*

On Relationships

Several times I have been asked whether Miss McCarty's life and acts are unique. Of course, one is always inclined to think that every life is unique and, certainly, Miss McCarty is very special. However, in another sense, I have come to regard Miss McCarty as a representative of many others who remain unsung.

Many correspondents have told Miss McCarty that she reminds them of someone important in their lives. One person described an immigrant mother who worked two or three jobs at a time to put her children through school. Another person described a church janitor who paid attention to a small boy in need of a friend. Several described maids or housekeepers that played important roles in their formative years. Somehow, Miss McCarty's story struck a chord in these people's lives, reminding them of that person from long ago.

Many of us, like those correspondents, had a special person in our lives as children — a person we respected, admired, and wanted to emulate. Sadly as we grew older and more sophisticated, we often stopped seeing those people through eyes of love and wonder. Where once heroes had stood, we found only ordinary people performing menial jobs.

I think Miss McCarty has reminded the whole country that all work can be performed with dignity and infused with quality. She reminds me, her friend and admirer, that I must be slow to dismiss anyone as unimportant.

— Paul Laughlin

I was an only child in a house
full of adults, so I didn't get into much
mischief. But if I did do something
wrong, my mother would spank me. She
lived her life before me as an example and
taught me the difference between right
and wrong. She also taught me the
consequences of misbehaving.

Most of the children take their habits from
the mother and father. They're going to try
to do what they see mama and daddy do.

*M*y grandmother was the closest thing I had to a hero as a child. She was sweet to me.

People tell me now that I am a hero, but I don't feel that way. I am nobody special. I am a plain, common person. I am no better than anybody else and I don't know everything. I don't want to be put up on a pedestal; I want to stay right here on the ground.

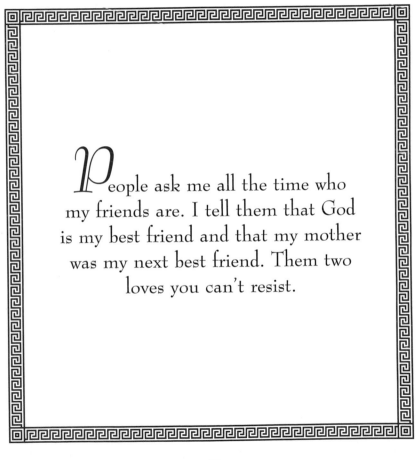

People ask me all the time who my friends are. I tell them that God is my best friend and that my mother was my next best friend. Them two loves you can't resist.

I had the advantage of two loving homes as a child. I moved back and forth between my grandmother's house and my uncle's. He was like a father to me, and I loved his children. We played well and they taught me how to do new things I had never tried. We got along all right. We were close. Family is the greatest blessing in this life.

My relatives were not lighthearted people, but I had a cousin who made me laugh all the time. She told silly stories like I had never heard before. I tell you, laughter is a good release. It's a blessing to be able to laugh at yourself.

*I*t is important to make special memories with the people you love. Everyday life fades from your mind, but it is easy to remember the celebrations and good times. I can't recall what we talked about on ordinary evenings, but I do remember Christmases spent with my mother, grandmother, and aunt. ⇒

During that season, they worked most nights babysitting or serving at parties. They usually came home around midnight loaded down with big plates of food. We would light the Christmas tree and sit down to a late dinner. At those times, we took joy in being together.

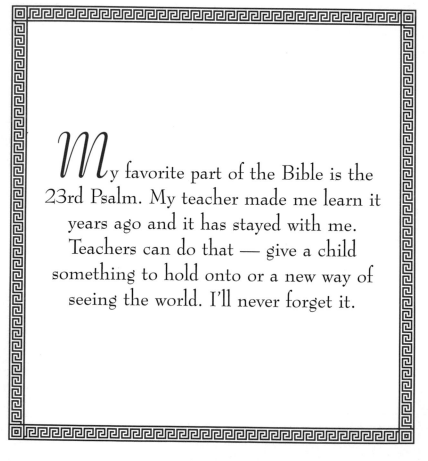

My favorite part of the Bible is the 23rd Psalm. My teacher made me learn it years ago and it has stayed with me. Teachers can do that — give a child something to hold onto or a new way of seeing the world. I'll never forget it.

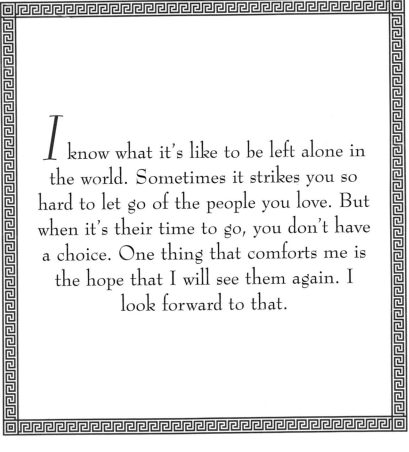

I know what it's like to be left alone in the world. Sometimes it strikes you so hard to let go of the people you love. But when it's their time to go, you don't have a choice. One thing that comforts me is the hope that I will see them again. I look forward to that.

I think that all people are equal but that doesn't mean that all people should have the same things. I don't think the Lord intends for everybody to have the same. Some have more and some have less; it's no cause to get jealous. You can have what you are willing to work and sacrifice for. But if somebody has more, that is no cause to think hard of that person. You have to learn to accept what you have.

$\mathcal{B}$uilding community is not that hard. It just takes ordinary friendliness. The woman who took me to the doctor when my arthritis got bad is a checkout person at my grocery store.

When she helped me with my groceries all those years, we spoke. I didn't stand there looking at the floor or the ceiling. We became acquainted.

McCarty returns to her Hattiesburg home after receiving an honorary degree from Harvard University, June 8, 1996. Photo by Jason Hurd.

On

Good

Living

The first television news crew to talk with Miss McCarty was a national network news team. Near the end of the interview, which had run long, the reporter asked her if he could take her shopping at her usual grocery store. He wanted film of her buying food.

The characteristically agreeable Miss McCarty said no. When the reporter asked why, she replied that she had bought all the groceries she needed the day before.

Trying another tack, the reporter suggested that they go to the store and *pretend* to be buying groceries. Again, she turned him down flat. She considered that plan dishonest.

Giving it one last try, the reporter proposed that they go to the store, film her buying whatever she wanted, and let him pick up the tab. She refused again.

Puzzled and slightly exasperated, the reporter asked why.

With the confidence of any clear-thinking, sensible person, Miss McCarty replied, "I just don't need any more groceries."

Needless to say, they never did make it to the store and that reporter learned a hard lesson about simplicity and no-nonsense thinking.

— Bud Kirkpatrick

We worked six days a week. Saturday was not especially different from any other day. My mother and aunt usually cooked for families in town and my grandmother spent the day catching up on her ironing. For my part, I washed and ironed my own clothes and cleaned the house for the rest of the week.

But Sundays were different. We took a day of rest. We attended church in the morning and the evening. It refreshed us for a new week. Everybody needs a day of rest.

I once took a trip to Niagara Falls. Law, the sound of the water was like the sound of the world coming to an end.

In the evenings we spread blankets on the ground and ate picnic dinners outdoors. I met people from all over the world.

On the return trip, we stopped in Chicago. I liked the city, but was ready to get back home. I missed the place where I belonged — where I was needed and making a contribution. No place, no matter how majestic, compares to the piece of earth where you have put down your roots.

Some people get angry about racial inequality and injustice, but I have no ill feeling toward white people. I just figure everybody is trying to make a living the best way they can. Washing and ironing was simply the way I had to make my living. I didn't mind because I didn't have an education. I think being educated is the way to live. That's God's best for us and that's the way to progress.

Loneliness is a terrible, terrible thing. I used to get so blue, I would just cry about it. Now I get to humming a song or I recite the 23rd Psalm. If you keep your mind occupied, Satan can't attack you. I try to keep my mind busy with work or the things I need to see to. I ain't got no time to be thinking about evil things.

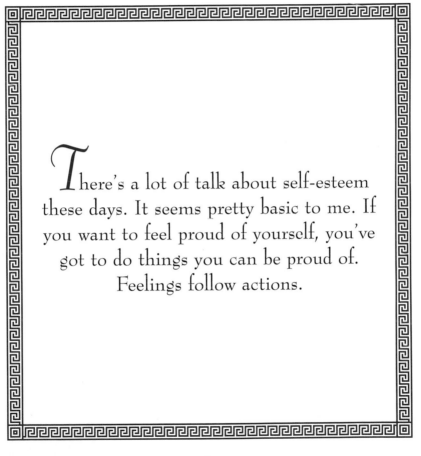

$\mathcal{T}$here's a lot of talk about self-esteem these days. It seems pretty basic to me. If you want to feel proud of yourself, you've got to do things you can be proud of. Feelings follow actions.

I stay in good health most of the time. I don't exercise too much, but work keeps me moving. I eat plenty of vegetables — carrots, beans, broccoli, cauliflower, and greens. I love to eat, but I eat in small amounts. If you don't eat too much, then you can eat whatever you want. Take a piece or a slice, not a whole or a half of something, with just a taste of tea. Too much tea is hard on your kidneys.

Worry can ruin you, so I try to keep it behind me. I keep busy with my work and let problems go on behind me or wherever they want to go. Let me press forward. My life is ahead of me. Sometimes the devil will overpower you with worry trying to keep you down and suck out all the good in your life. You've got to be careful and guard your thoughts because he'll tell you lies that look like the truth.

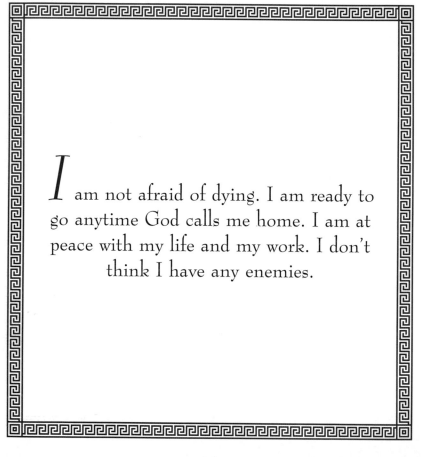

I am not afraid of dying. I am ready to go anytime God calls me home. I am at peace with my life and my work. I don't think I have any enemies.

*I*t upsets me to see so many people suing for big amounts of money. Most of the time what happens is just an accident. I don't understand people wanting to take advantage and get something for nothing. When people come into money that way, they usually fall out of it just as fast.

When I was a girl, few colored people had telephones. My aunt and grandmother worked in white people's houses, and they would use the phones there to call the store and order our groceries for delivery. They didn't have to spend time running back and forth. Life was ordered. We didn't have the benefit of computers, but we had more peacefulness. Our minds and bodies need that.

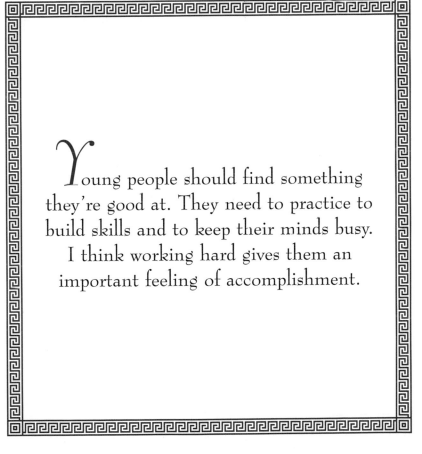

$\mathcal{Y}$oung people should find something they're good at. They need to practice to build skills and to keep their minds busy. I think working hard gives them an important feeling of accomplishment.

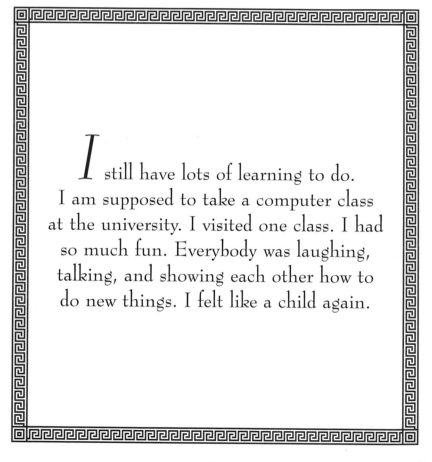

I still have lots of learning to do.
I am supposed to take a computer class
at the university. I visited one class. I had
so much fun. Everybody was laughing,
talking, and showing each other how to
do new things. I felt like a child again.

When I leave this world, I can't take nothing away from here. I'm old and I won't live always — that's why I gave the money to the school and put my affairs in order. I planned it and I am proud of it. I am proud that I worked hard and that my money will help young people who have worked hard to deserve it. I'm proud that I am leaving something positive in this world. My only regret is that I didn't have more to give.

Springtime is my favorite season. I love the soft rain. Everything is beautiful coming into leaf and bloom. That's my idea of paradise.

My grandmother kept a nice garden around the house. Our yard was full of flowers. The sight of them was comforting; it filled me with hope.

I do have a few fears. I am afraid of the dark and I am scared to death of snakes and lizards. I don't enjoy taking fish off the hook. But I don't let those things keep me from living.

After my aunt died, leaving me alone, I hardly slept for three months. I had always been the littlest thing in the house, but the time came for me to grow up. I did.

I try to keep things as simple and organized as possible. I go to the store once a week for my groceries. I buy clothes once or twice a year. If something like detergent comes in two sizes, I buy the larger one. I don't want to be running back and forth to the store when I could be working or relaxing. I don't like all that rushing around.

Some people make a lot of noise about what's wrong with the world, and they are usually blaming somebody else. I think people who don't like the way things are need to look at themselves first. They need to get right with God and change their own ways. That way, they will know that they are making a difference in at least one life. If everybody did that, we'd be all right.

THE OSEOLA McCARTY SCHOLARSHIP

Students are selected for the Oseola McCarty Scholarship by the Financial Aid Office at the University of Southern Mississippi. The criteria for selection include financial need, satisfactory grades, and leadership. Preference is given to African-American students from the Hattiesburg, Mississippi, area.

The USM Foundation, which is a 501(c)(3) non-profit organization, administers the scholarship. Donations may be sent to the USM Foundation, Box 10026, Hattiesburg, MS 39406. Please make checks payable to the foundation and designate the Oseola McCarty Scholarship on the check.